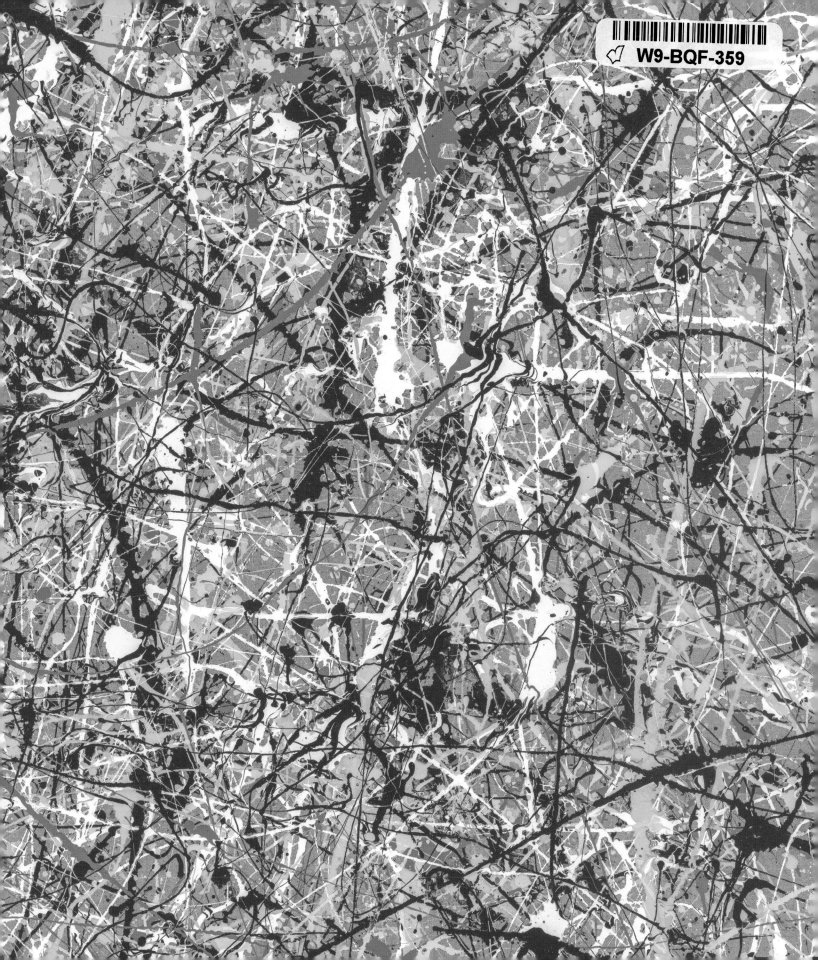

If *Picasso* painted a SNOWMAN

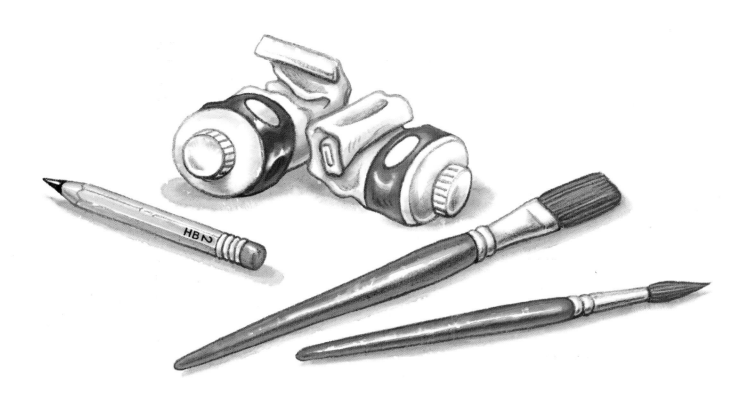

For Dean, Joan, Claris, and Jodean—thank you for Paris and so much more.
To Josie, Daniel, and Will—you are the reason.
—A.N.

In memory of Carol and Murray Tinkelman, who
helped me believe I could create a masterpiece.
—G.N.

And in memory of Rick Walton, who helped us begin.
—A.N. & G.N.

Tilbury House Publishers
12 Starr Street
Thomaston, Maine 04861
800-582-1899 • www.tilburyhouse.com

Hardcover ISBN 978-088448-593-3
ebook ISBN 978-0-88448-595-7

First hardcover printing September 2017

15 16 17 18 19 20 XXX 10 9 8 7 6 5 4

Library of Congress Control Number: 2017941519

Cover and interior design by Frame25 Productions

Printed in Korea

If *Picasso* painted a
SNOWMAN

AMY & GREG NEWBOLD

TILBURY HOUSE PUBLISHERS, THOMASTON, MAINE

If someone asked you to paint a snowman, you would probably start with three white circles stacked one upon another.

Then you would add black dots for eyes, an orange triangle for a nose, and a black dotted smile.

But if Pablo Picasso painted a snowman it would look like . . .

THIS!

Not all artists paint the same.

Can you find J.M.W. Turner's snowman . . .

lost in the blizzard?

BLAM!
Roy Lichtenstein's snow hero saves the day!

Georgia O'Keeffe's snowman wouldn't bloom long in the desert.

A patchwork quilt,
soft and cozy, wraps
up Gustav Klimt's
snow family.

How many snowmen hide in Claude Monet's haystacks?

A dust-colored snowman watches
Pablita Velarde's ornamental birds.

Jackson Pollock
painted his snowman . . .

SPLISH,
SPLASH,
SPLAT!

In Salvador Dali's winter fantasy, snowmen drip like melty cheese.

Rickety-rack! A stick snowman drives
Paul Klee's wire car.

Marc Chagall's snowmen cavort in a bright circus ring.

Dot
Upon
Dot
Upon
Dot,

here's a snowman by
Georges Seurat!

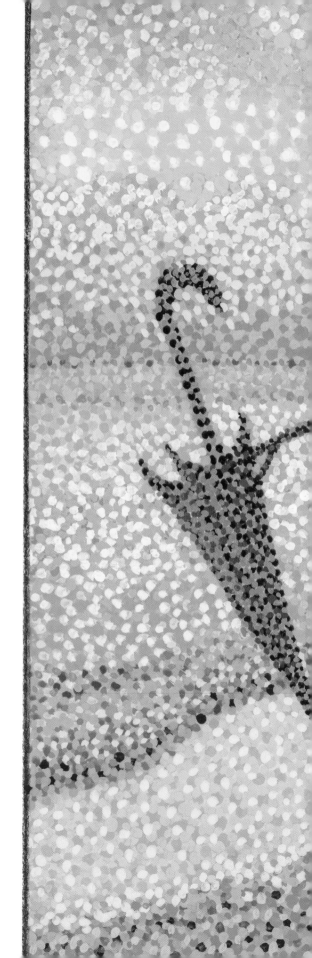

Piet Mondrian's snowman is square.
Do you see a carrot
anywhere there?

Circles surround circles as Sonia
Delaunay's snowman spins.

The rhythms of
the street make
Jacob Lawrence's
snowman smile.

Vincent van Gogh's snowman swirls
and curls in the wavy hills.

And Grant Wood's famous
Snowman Gothic will never melt away.

What would your snowman look like?

Copy this page and make your own.

Meet the Artists

None of the artists in this book painted a snowman, but the snowmen they could have painted might have looked like these. All of these artists learned the basics of drawing and painting and studied the work of other great artists before developing their own styles. None of them ever quit.

 **Pablo Picasso** (1881–1973) was born in Spain but moved to France as a young man. After learning how to paint things that looked real, he set out to make his art original. He painted mainly with blues and greens for years, then switched to pinks and reds. He began deconstructing people and objects into shapes that he rearranged in new ways. This style of art became known as Cubism. He worked hard to paint with childlike imagination. He said, "There is no abstract art. One must always begin with something. Afterwards one can remove all semblance of reality."

 **Joseph Mallord William Turner** (1775–1851) signed his paintings "J.M.W. Turner," but his family called him William. Painting landscapes when most other English painters were portraying historical scenes, he began leaving out details of objects, focusing instead on the interplay of light and shadow through clouds, in storms, and across water and land. His moody paintings inspired Claude Monet and the Impressionists. William once said, "If there were anything to be had in nature blacker than black, I'd use it."

 **Roy Lichtenstein** (1923–1997) would often change the focus of previously printed images in his art. A sci-fi and comic book fan as a kid in New York, he would zoom in on part of a comic and create his own picture. He developed a version of Ben-Day—dots of four colors applied with a stencil—to add texture to his paintings and create illusions of shading and blended colors, similar to Seurat's Pointillism. He and other artists elevated commercial art into the pop art of the gallery world.

Georgia O'Keeffe (1887–1986) once wrote, "I could say things with color and shapes that I couldn't say in any other way, things that I had no words for." She painted small details of flowers very large. "Nobody sees a flower, really," she said. "It is so small it takes time. We haven't time, and to see takes time, like to have a friend takes time." She loved the desert scenery of New Mexico, her adopted home. Georgia's paintings of flowers, skulls, mountain peaks, and skyscrapers blazed a trail for American modernist painting.

Gustav Klimt (1862–1918) was born in Austria, one of seven children of poor immigrant parents. His early work creating murals for public buildings influenced his art. Gustav was a Symbolist painter, trying to convey meaning through shapes and colors. His paintings had a dreamy quality and were filled with lines and patterns. In Gustav's "Golden" phase, he used gold leaf in his paintings, inspired by old Byzantine pictures.

Claude Monet (1840–1926) grew up in Le Havre, France. "School was always like a prison to me," he said. "I doodled in the margins of my books . . . and drew the faces and profiles of my schoolmasters as outrageously as I could." After being introduced to *plein air* paint-ing—painting outdoors—he helped pioneer the style of painting called Impressionism, using short brush strokes and bright colors rather than smooth strokes and carefully blended colors. Later in life he would paint the same scenes—haystacks, a cathedral, water lilies—many times in varying light and from different angles.

Pablita Velarde (1918–2006) was a Native American artist born in Santa Clara Pueblo, New Mexico. Her birth name, Tse Tsan, means "Golden Dawn." Her mother died when she was three years old. When she was six, her father sent her to St. Catherine's Indian School in Santa Fe, where she began drawing and painting. An elder told her to stop, because Pueblo tradition did not allow women to paint, but Pablita kept on. Her paintings show Pueblo life in great detail in her signature "flat" style. "Have faith in yourself," she said, "otherwise it just won't come out of you."

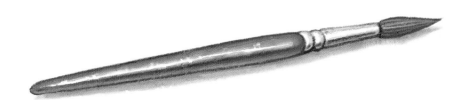

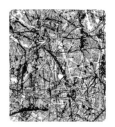**Jackson Pollock** (1912–1956) grew up in the American Southwest. His father was a road surveyor in the Grand Canyon region, where Jackson soaked up the dramatic scenery. He became famous for his "drip" paintings, part of the Abstract Expressionist movement. He would place a large canvas on the floor so that he could work from any side of it, as he had seen Native American artists do in their sand paintings. He would then drip or splash paint onto the canvas using sticks instead of brushes. Jackson said, "The painting has a life of its own. I try to let it come through."

**Salvador Dali** (1904–1989) once said, "Begin by drawing and painting like the old masters. After that do as you see fit—you will always be respected." Salvador daydreamed in school in Spain. He dressed in crazy fashions and imitated the famous painter Diego Velázquez with the long, curving mustache that he wore throughout his adult life. Salvador experimented with Cubism but became a Surrealist—a movement that sought to bring forth images from the subconscious—and began producing art based on his dreams. One of his most famous paintings, of melting clocks, is titled *The Persistence of Memory*.

**Paul Klee** (1879–1940) could draw and paint with either hand. Fascinated by abstract art and influenced by the intense light and colors of North Africa, the Swiss painter worked in the Cubist, Expressionist, and Surrealist styles, striving to achieve a childlike creativity. He saw connections between music, art, and words, writing in his diary, "All things an artist must be: poet, explorer of nature, philosopher!" Paul invented a technique called oil-transfer drawing, which produces ragged, primitive-looking lines.

Marc Chagall (1887–1985) was born as Moische Segal into a poor family in a small town in Russia. In 1910 he moved to Paris, changing his name. He painted blue cows and a violinist with a green face. People floated and soared across his canvases. When the Nazis occupied Paris in the 1940s, many of his paintings were confiscated or destroyed because he was Jewish. "The stars were my best friends," he said. "The air was full of legends and phantoms, full of mythical and fairy-tale creatures, which suddenly flew away over the roof, so that one was at one with the firmament."

Georges Seurat (1859–1891) was fascinated by color. The Parisian painter placed dots of complementary colors side by side rather than mixing paints to achieve a desired color. Today his technique is called Pointillism. Georges' most famous painting, *Sunday Afternoon on the Island of Grand Jatte,* is seven feet tall and ten feet wide and took him two years to complete. Georges died at the age of thirty-one. He once said that people "see poetry in what I have done. No. I apply my method and that is all there is to it."

Piet Mondrian (1872–1944) was born in Holland and painted landscapes in the traditional Dutch style. Then he began to emphasize the lines he saw in landscapes and objects. Using primary colors with black lines, painting squares and rectangles, he worked to free his art from the objects it represented. "When I construct lines and color combinations on a flat surface," he said, "it is with the aim of portraying universal beauty as consciously as possible." Piet called his style Neoplasticism.

Sonia Delaunay (1906–1979) was born as Sarah Stern into a poor Jewish family in Ukraine. When she was five years old, her parents sent Sonia (her nickname) to live with an aunt and uncle in St. Petersburg, Russia, where she began studying art. She left Russia at age eighteen and later moved to Paris. Sonia painted marketplaces and Flamenco performers in Spain and became famous for her work in fashion. She and her husband, Robert Delaunay, founded an art style called Orphism, which grew out of Cubism but emphasized bright colors and overlapping geometric shapes. Sonia said, "I have always changed everything around me. I have lived my art."

Jacob Lawrence (1917–2000) lived in foster homes in New Jersey after his parents separated, until his mother found work and they moved to New York City. There Jacob was surrounded by the writers and artists of the Harlem Renaissance. In 1940 he began a series of paintings documenting the twentieth-century migration of millions of African-Americans (including Jacob's parents) from America's rural south to the urban north in search of a better life. *The Migration of the Negro* series of sixty paintings is remarkable for the vibrancy and movement Jacob achieved with a limited color palette and dynamic shapes.

Vincent van Gogh (1853–1890), born in the Netherlands, did not create his first notable painting, *The Potato Eaters*, until 1885. Influenced by the Impressionists and Japanese art, Vincent developed a Post-Impressionist style that featured a wide variety of colors and thick swathes of paint applied with bold brush strokes. "I long so much to make beautiful things," he wrote to his brother, Theo. Despite struggling with mental illness—which once caused him to mutilate his left ear—he created 860 oil paintings of sunflowers, irises, the French countryside, people, and self-portraits in the last few years before he ended his life at age thirty-seven. *The Starry Night* is among history's most beloved paintings. Only one of his paintings sold during his lifetime, but today they are worth millions of dollars.

 **Grant Wood** (1891–1942) was born on a farm in Iowa. His father died when he was ten, and his mother took the children to the city of Cedar Rapids, where Grant escaped into art. In 1928 he had the chance to visit Germany, where he studied the work of German and Flemish painters. Upon returning home, he painted his sister and his dentist in front of a Gothic window in a farmhouse, making them tall and thin to mimic the window. This painting, known as *American Gothic*, became famous. His paintings of rolling Iowa hills and scenes of farm life helped start a new art tradition called American Regionalism.

Greg Newbold's Advice for Artists

*Developing your unique artistic style and voice
takes work, so keep practicing. Here are three tips:*

1. Draw.
Drawing is magic, and it's the best way to improve your art. Try to draw exactly what you see. Look for big shapes before you add details. Draw an object from different angles to develop perspective. Carry a sketchbook and draw all the time. Once you can draw realistically, you will be able to make real objects look however you want. Simplify shapes. Stylize and distort things. Merge objects for fun.

2. Explore.
Artists undertake long journeys to discover their styles. On your journey, experiment with acrylic paints, watercolors, charcoals, pastel chalks, colored pencils, or oil paints. Try surfaces like paper, canvas, cardboard, metal, or wood. Combine materials and methods to find out how they respond to each other. Maybe you will like painting on collaged magazine clippings or printed fabric. Glue objects into your art and paint around or on top of them.

3. Have Fun!
With each color or brush stroke you apply, let the picture suggest what to do next. Trust your vision. There is no right or wrong way to make art, only ways that work or don't work. If your picture doesn't turn out quite the way you wanted, figure out what worked well and use that knowledge in the future. Be inspired by other artists, but don't compare your work with theirs. They are not you!

Good luck on your artistic journey!

AMY NEWBOLD grew up drawing horses. While visiting the Musée Picasso in Paris, she wondered what a snowman painted by Picasso would look like. Although she once fell asleep in an art history class, she has always loved art, museums, and museum gift shops. Before writing this book, Amy would have drawn a snowman by stacking three white circles one upon another, but now she is planning to paint a snowman made of dots. Amy loves road trips with her husband Greg, writing, and hiking and camping in the mountains near her home.

Award-winning illustrator GREG NEWBOLD grew up drawing superheroes and Dr. Seuss characters on giant end rolls of newsprint in his childhood basement. He once copied a Vincent van Gogh painting for a college art history class instead of writing a paper. Greg found it challenging and fun to paint in the styles of so many of his favorite artists for this book. He loves his job of making pictures and has illustrated a dozen books for children. In his free time, Greg enjoys gardening, fishing, road trips with Amy, and painting the natural wonders near his Utah home.

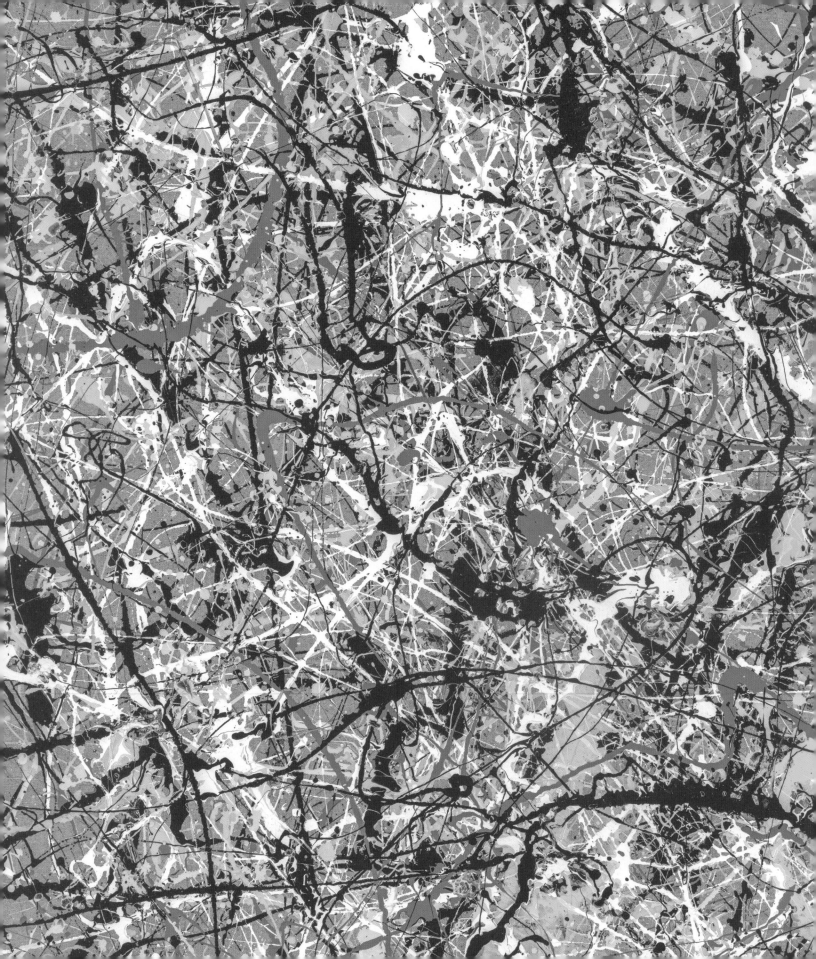